Wonderful
WORLD 1
WORKBOOK

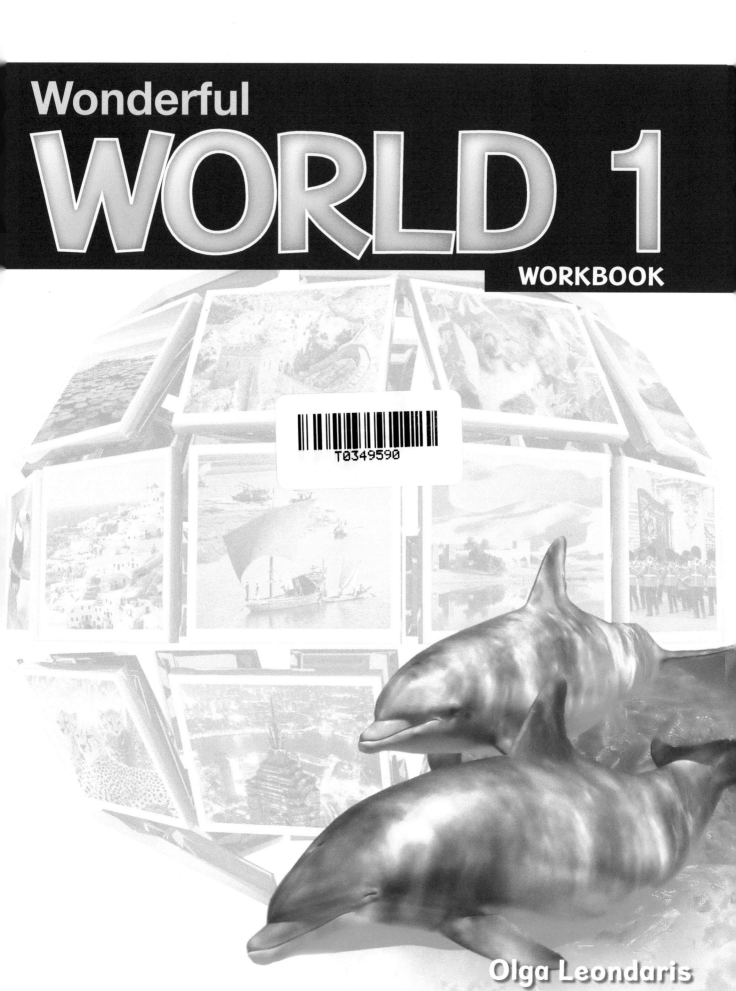

Olga Leondaris

Wonderful World 1 Workbook
Olga Leondaris

Publisher: Jason Mann

Director of Content Development: Sarah Bideleux

Commissioning Editor: Carol Goodwright

Development Editor: Lynn Thomson

Assistant Editor: Manuela Barros

Content Project Editor: Amy Smith

Art Director: Natasa Arsenidou

Cover Designer: Vasiliki Christoforidou

Text designer: Tania Diakaki

Compositor: Rouli Manias

National Geographic Editorial Liaison: Leila Hishmeh

Acknowledgements

Illustrated by George Melissaropoulos, Theodoros Piakis and Panagiotis Angeletakis

The publisher would like to thank the following sources for permission to reproduce their copyright protected images:
iStockphoto – pp24 (Karen Hogan), 25 (Eva Serrabassa), 47 (Ekaterina Monakhova), 71 (Joshua Blake), 73 (Ronald Bloom); **National Geographic** – pp 82 iii (Jason Edwards), 101 i (John Weaver), 101 ii (David Doubilet), 103 i (Panoramic Images) ii (Richard Nowitz); **Photolibrary Group** – p23 (Cultura); **Thinkstock** – pp46 (iStockphoto), 53 (iStockphoto), 74tc (Hemera Technologies). All other photos courtesy of Shutterstock.

ISBN: 978-1-111-40067-5

National Geographic Learning
Cheriton House
North Way
Andover
Hampshire
SP10 5BE
United Kingdom

Cengage Learning is a leading provider of customized learning solutions with office locations around the globe, including Singapore, the United Kingdom, Australia, Mexico, Brazil and Japan. Locate your local office at: **international.cengage.com/region**

Cengage Learning products are represented in Canada by Nelson Education, Ltd.

Visit National Geographic Learning online at **ngl.cengage.com**

Visit our corporate website at **www.cengage.com**

Printed in the United Kingdom by Ashford Colour Press
Print Number 13 Print Year 2020

Contents

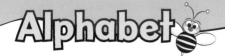

Alphabet

A   Match.

A   B   C   D

d   b   a   c

B   Write A, B, C or D.

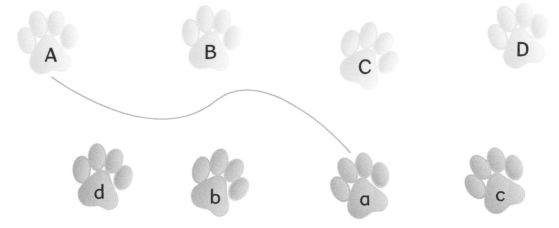

C   Write and say.

What's your name?

My name's
_____.

A Circle e, f, g and h.

B Find and circle.

F	R	O	G	G
E	A	F	B	I
G	H	A	T	R
G	C	E	D	L

C Colour, write and say.

Hello. ___How___ are you?

_____, thank you.

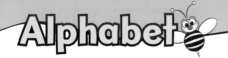

Alphabet

A **Match.**

I   J   K   L

k   l   j   i

B **Circle.**

a o n **king** j l o i n s e c t e n s i l e m o n k u l j u g e m

C **Write and say.**

What's your ___name___?

My name's Jane.

_____ are you?

Fine, _____ you.

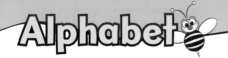

A Circle m, n, o and p.

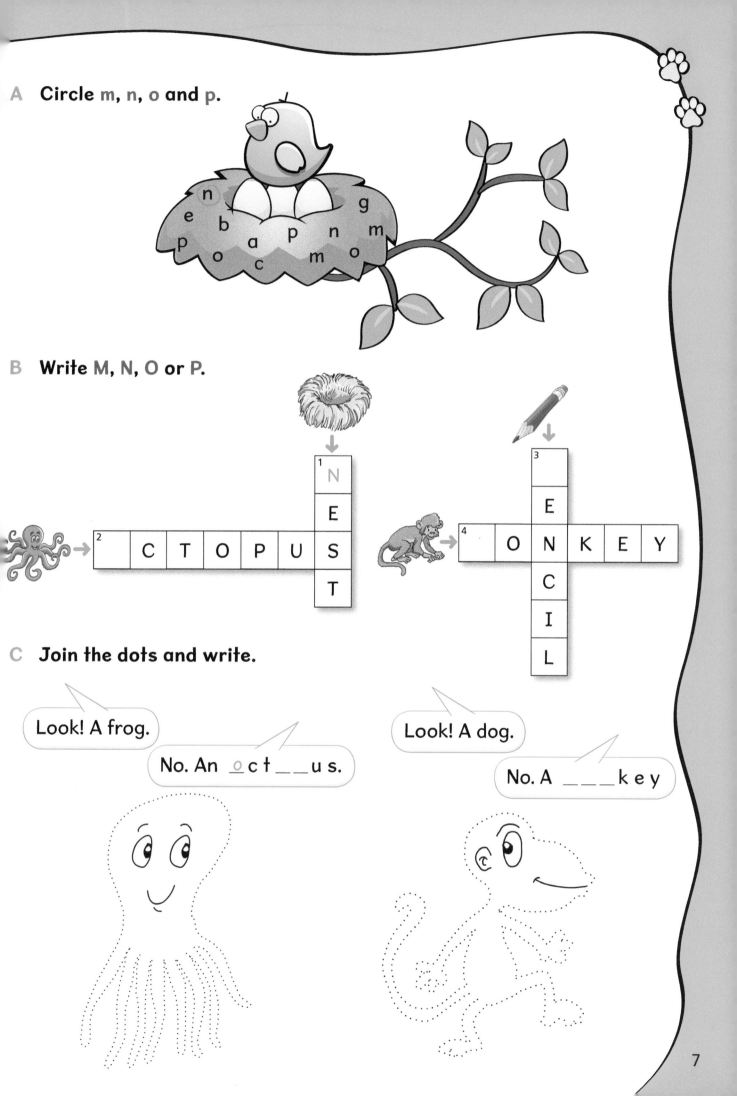

B Write M, N, O or P.

1. N E S T

2. _ C T O P U S

3. _ E _ O N K E Y with P E N C I L

C Join the dots and write.

Look! A frog.

No. An _o_ c t _ _ u s.

Look! A dog.

No. A _ _ _ _ k e y

7

Alphabet

A Match.

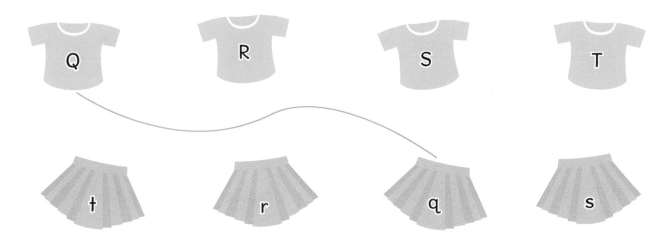

B Circle.

s p i t i g e r q u o s p i d e r r i g q u i l t d e r r o b o t l t

C Write and say.

_____Here_____ you are, Amber.
Thanks. Thanks. _____ .
You're _____ , Amber.
A spider! _____ !

A Write.

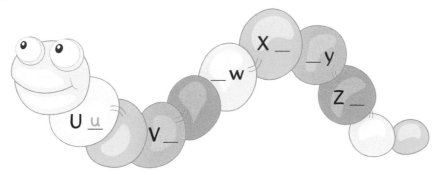

U u   V _   _ w   X _   _ y   Z _

B Find and circle.

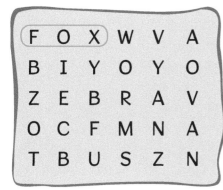

F O X W V A
B I Y O Y O
Z E B R A V
O C F M N A
T B U S Z N

C Colour and say.

Goodbye! Thank you!

Bye! You're welcome!

Alphabet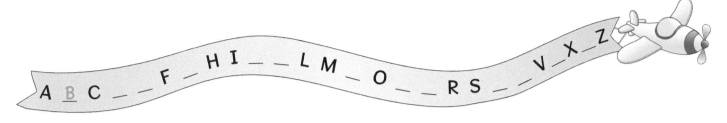

A **Write.**

A _B_ C _ _ _ F _ H I _ _ _ L M _ O _ _ R S _ _ V _ X _ Z

_ b _ d e _ g _ _ _ j k _ _ _ n _ p q _ _ _ t u _ w _ y _

B **Write and say.**

A B C D E F G

A _ _ _ _ _ _ _

Sing everybody!
Sing everybody!
Sing the alphabet song!

H I J K L M N

_ _ _ _ _ _ _

Sing everybody!
Sing everybody!
Sing the alphabet song!

O P Q R S T U

_ _ _ _ _ _ _

V and W

_ and _

_ _ _

Colours

A Match.

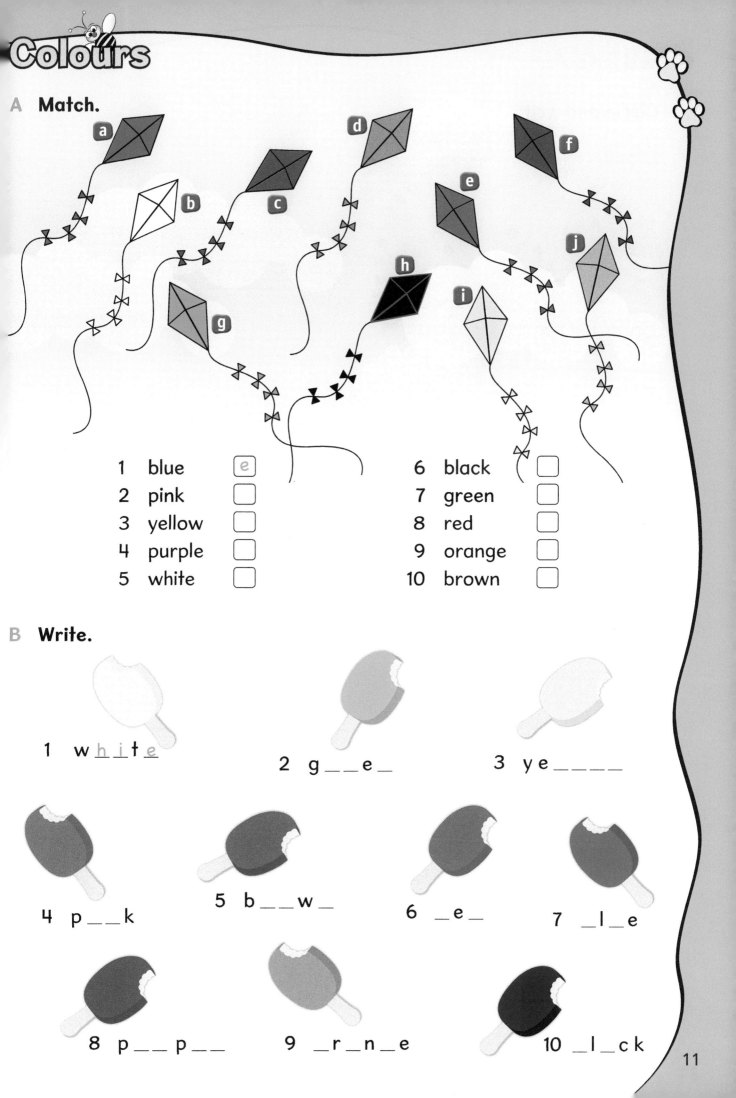

1 blue	e	6 black ☐
2 pink ☐		7 green ☐
3 yellow ☐		8 red ☐
4 purple ☐		9 orange ☐
5 white ☐		10 brown ☐

B Write.

1 w <u>h i t e</u>

2 g _ _ e _

3 y e _ _ _ _ _

4 p _ _ k

5 b _ _ w _

6 _ e _

7 _ l _ e

8 p _ _ p _ _

9 _ r _ n _ e

10 _ l _ c k

11

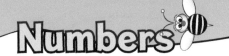
Numbers

A Circle and write.

onemitwodthreefhpfourqgfiveksixtus...
znineatenrtye
xeightjz
venxeight

one _____ _____
_____ _____
_____ _____
_____ _____
_____ _____

B Match.

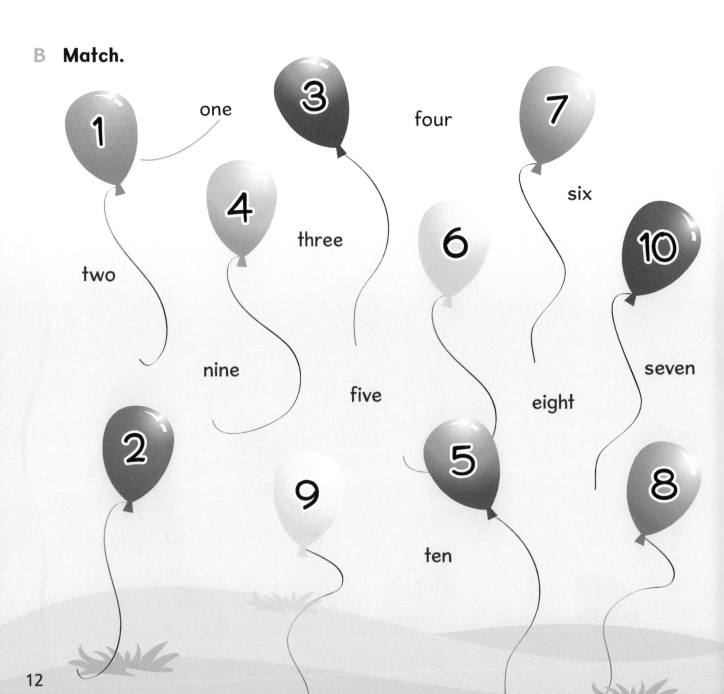

one

two

three

four

six

nine

five

eight

seven

ten

A **Write.**

 M i a

 _ y

 L _ _

 _ r _ k

B **Match and say.**

What's your name?

How old are you?

How are you?

Fine, thanks.

My name's Trek.

I'm nine.

Lesson 1

A Circle.

baby / elephant

mum / fly

photo / mum

fly / elephant

photo / baby

B Write.

1 f l y

2 e _ e _ _ a _ t

3 _ u _

4 b _ _ _ _

5 p _ o _ o

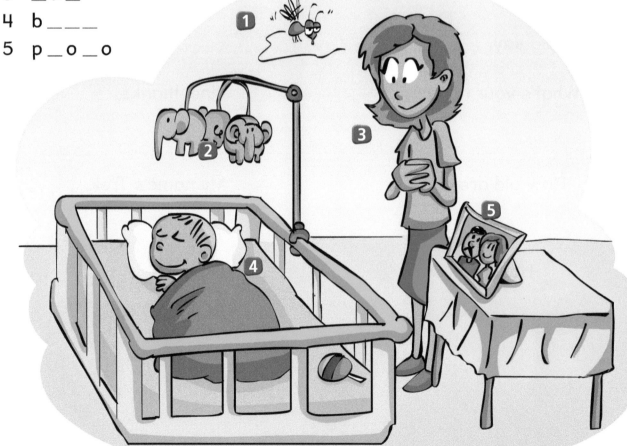

C **Write.**

ant   baby   egg   elephant   fly   hat
insect   monkey   octopus   photo

a

baby
_____
_____
_____
_____

an

ant
_____
_____
_____
_____

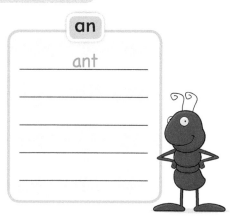

D **Join the dots and write.**

1
2
3

a spider
_____   _____   _____

4
5

_____   _____

E **Join the dots. Then write and say.**

Wow! A _f_ antastic
ele _ _ _ ant!

15

Lesson 2

A **Match.**

igloo
family
house
brother
dad
sister

B **Find, circle and write.**

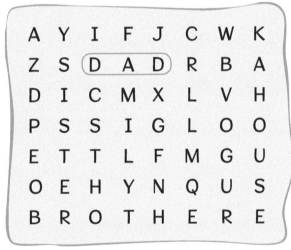

```
A  Y  I  F  J  C  W  K
Z  S (D  A  D) R  B  A
D  I  C  M  X  L  V  H
P  S  S  I  G  L  O  O
E  T  T  L  F  M  G  U
O  E  H  Y  N  Q  U  S
B  R  O  T  H  E  R  E
```

dad

_____

_____

_____

_____

_____

C Circle.

1 My brother (is) / are three years old.
2 You am / are great!
3 The house are / is fantastic.
4 My family am / is cool!
5 The baby are / is a boy!
6 I am / is nine years old.

D Write 'm, 're or 's.

1 I _____'m_____ a girl.
2 He _____ a hunter.
3 It _____ an igloo.
4 You _____ eight years old.
5 She _____ my sister.
6 I _____ cool!

E Write and say.

My f a m i l y is cool.
My _ _ m _ l _ is great.
So come on and celebrate!

Mum is c _ o _ .
Dad is _ o _ l
B _ _ t _ _ rs and _ i _ _ er _
We're so co _ _ _ !

17

A **Match.**

My mum is cool.
My grandpa is great.
My best friend is seven.
My grandma is nice.

B **Circle.**

p o g r e a t l o b e s t f r i e n d e s t n i c e

v c a g r a n d m a y p

w a s g r a n d p a o b

C **Write.**

1	We are best friends.	_____We're_____ best friends.
2	They are brothers.	_____ brothers.
3	You are great!	_____ great!
4	We are eight years old.	_____ eight years old.
5	You are my best friend.	_____ my best friend.
6	They are nice!	_____ nice!

D **Write.**

| They're best friends. | ~~They're monkeys.~~ | You're my grandma. |
| You're my grandpa. | We're brothers. | We're sisters. |

_____ They're _____ monkeys.

E **Write and say.**

am   from   ~~name~~   years

Hi! My ___name___ is Zina. I _____ seven _____ old. I am _____ Africa.

Lesson 1

A Circle.

1

(tall) / short

2

lion / giraffe

3

camera / giraffe

4

lion / camera

5

short / tall

6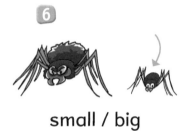

small / big

B Match.

1

2

3

4

5

6

7

8

a tall giraffe
a short giraffe
a big lion
a small lion
a big camera
a small camera
a tall boy
a short boy

C Write.

elephant ~~giraffe~~ monkey lion tiger zebra

1

giraffe   giraffes

4

_____   _____

2

_____   _____

5

_____   _____

3

_____   _____

6

_____   _____

D Circle and colour.

1 one / (three) hats

2 one / two yo-yo

3 one / four egg

4 one / five cars

E Write and say.

Sam is my <u>s</u> i _ ter.
_ _ e's _ ix.
_ _ e's _ _ ort.

21

Lesson 2

A **Write.**

1 t <u>o</u> y <u>s</u>

2 r _ b _ t

3 c _ m _ u _ e _ ga _ e

4 b _ ll

5 _ ka _ e _ o _ _ d

B **Match.**

computer games   robots   balls   toys   skateboards

C **Write.**

1 you / tall / aren't   You aren't tall.

2 a / isn't / skateboard / it _____

3 hats / aren't / big / they   _____

4 aren't / girls / we   _____

5 isn't / he / short   _____

D Write.

It's a skateboard.

1

It isn't a skateboard.

4

It's big.

_____

2

They're dogs.

_____

5
We're friends.

_____

3

I'm a girl.

_____

6
They're photos.

_____

E Write and say.

1 It isn't big. It's green.
   It's a skateboard.

2 It isn't small. It's red.
   _____

3 It isn't yellow. It's big and blue.
   _____

4 It isn't red. It's big and green.
   _____

23

Lesson 3

A   Read and draw.

A birthday cake | A teddy bear | A present

B   Write.

C Circle.

1 Is it a robot? (Yes, it is.)/ No, it isn't.

2 Are they balls? Yes, they are. / No, they aren't.

3 Is she happy? Yes, she is. / No, she isn't.

4 Is the boy tall? Yes, he is. / No, he isn't.

5 Is it a teddy bear? Yes, it is. / No, it isn't.

D Write.

1 __Are__ you short?
Yes, I ___am___ .

2 _____ Mike ten years old?
No, he _____ .

3 _____ it a teddy bear?
Yes, it _____ .

4 _____ I tall?
No, you _____ .

5 _____ we best friends?
Yes, we _____ .

E Write and say.

H _a_ _p_ _p_ y B _ _ _ _ _ _ _ y, Tina. Here you are.

Wow! A t _ _ _ _ y b_ _ r. Thanks, Bill

You're w_ _ _ _ _ _ e.

Lesson 1

A Write.

beach bird mountain ostrich penguin whale

1 _____beach_____

2 _____

3 _____

4 _____

5 _____

6 _____

B Find, circle and write.

M	O	U	N	T	A	I	N	D	P
D	S	A	A	B	M	M	I	F	E
C	T	R	G	G	Y	H	Y	K	N
U	R	T	O	B	I	R	D	P	G
I	I	R	D	E	W	H	A	L	U
N	C	F	D	A	X	A	B	N	I
P	H	J	L	C	P	C	W	R	N
H	H	E	M	H	Y	S	S	L	S
N	E	A	C	H	K	O	P	P	I
P	E	N	G	W	H	A	L	E	S

_____mountain_____

_____

_____

_____

_____

_____

26

C Circle.

1 (This is) / That's a beach.

2 This is / That's an ostrich.

3 This is / That's an egg.

4 This is / That's a whale.

5 This is / That's a mountain.

6 This is / That's a penguin.

D Write This is or That's.

1 ____That's____ a bird. It's brown!
2 _____ a cake. It's pink!
3 _____ a teddy bear. It's blue!
4 _____ a penguin. It's black and white!

E Colour. Then write and say.

The ostri _c h_ is in the __ ar. The __ ar is on the bea ___ . __ool!

27

3 Lesson 2

A Match.

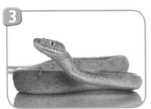

animals
food
hungry
lizard
meerkat
snake

B Write.

C Circle.

1 These / (Those) are meerkats.
2 These / Those are lizards.
3 These / Those are boys.
4 These / Those are snakes.
5 These / Those are teddy bears.

D Write These or Those.

1 _____Those_____ are hats.
2 _____ are pencils.
3 _____ are cameras.

4 _____ are photos.
5 _____ are DVDs.
6 _____ are flowers.

E Write and say.

I'm a s n a k e – hiss hiss!
I'm a snake – hiss h _ _ s!
I'm a snake, I'm a snake, I'm a snake!

I'm a l _ _ _ n – roar roar!
I'm a lion – r _ _ _ r roar!
I'm a lion, I'm a lion, I'm a lion!

I'm a p _ _ _ _ _ _ n – wobble wobble!
I'm a penguin – w _ _ _ _ _ e wobble!
I'm a penguin, I'm a penguin, I'm penguin!

A Circle.

lopdolphinssharkfrtyrabbitwatreepqrbivspfflowerbd

B Join the dots and write.

1

tree

2

_____

3

_____

4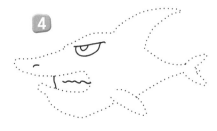

_____

5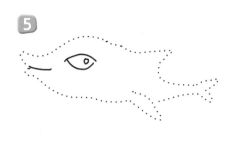

_____

C Match.

1

2

What are those?
What are these?
What's this?
What's that?

3

4

30

D Circle and write.

1 What's this / (that)?

_____It's_____ a snake.

2 What are these / those?

_____ animals.

3 What's this / that?

_____ an ostrich.

4 What are these / those?

_____ mountains.

5 What's this / that?

_____ a present.

E Write and say.

1 What's this?

It's _____a dolphin_____ .

2 What's this?

It's _____ .

3 What's this?

It's _____ .

4 What's this?

It's _____ .

5 What's this?

It's _____ .

6 What's this?

It's _____ .

31

Review 1 🐝

A **Find, circle and write.**

D	T	P	P	S	W	B	A	L	L
O	E	E	G	K	W	I	W	G	R
L	D	N	R	A	B	J	X	G	A
P	D	G	A	T	Q	S	O	I	B
H	Y	U	N	E	G	H	R	R	B
I	B	I	D	B	T	A	B	A	I
N	E	N	P	O	L	R	A	F	T
E	A	M	A	A	I	K	M	F	B
F	R	Z	B	R	O	T	H	E	R
T	M	U	M	D	N	K	O	Y	M

Animals, Birds and Fish

giraffe _____ _____

_____ _____

_____ _____

Family

_____

_____

Toys

_____

_____

B **Circle and write.**

1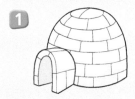
a / an   igloo

2
a / an _____

3
a / an _____

4
a / an _____

5
a / an _____

6
a / an _____

C **Circle.**

1   What are those? It's / They're flowers.

2   What are these? It's / They're teddy bears.

3   What's this? It's / They're a camera.

4   What's that? It's / They're a birthday cake.

5   What are these? It's / They're drawings.

6   What's this? It's / They're a DVD.

D Write.

I'm not   It isn't   She isn't   They're   We're   He's

____I'm not____ hungry.   _____ a baby.   _____ tall.

_____ teddy
bears.   _____ a beach.   _____ best
friends.

E Write.

1 Are you short?   Yes, _____I am_____ .
2 Is she cool?   No, _____ .
3 Are they brothers?   Yes, _____ .
4 Are we best friends? Yes, _____ .
5 Is it a birthday cake? No, _____ .
6 Is he hungry?   No, _____ .

F Write.

She is my mum. She is nice.   He is my dad. He is tall.
They are my brothers. They are cool!

1 They are my brothers.
   They are cool!

2 _____

   _____

3 _____

   _____

Lesson 1

A Match.

drawing
helicopter
pupil
school

B Write.

1 **16** s i x t e e n

2 **15** f _ f _ _ e _

3 **17** se _ _ _ _ t e _ n

4 **12** _ w e _ _ e

5 **13** t _ _ r _ ee _

6 **11** _ l e _ en

C Circle.

1 There's / There are two schools.
2 There's / There are nineteen pupils.
3 There's / There are a black spider.
4 There's / There are a big present for you!
5 There's / There are four teddy bears.
6 There's / There are a nest in that tree.

D **Write There's or There are.**

1 _____There's_____ a pupil.

4 _____ a tree.

2 _____ two dogs.

5 _____ a helicopter.

3 _____ six teddy bears.

6 _____ three dolphins.

E **Colour. Then write and say.**

1 There's a spid _e r_ in a hat.

2 There's a tig __ __ in a tree.

Lesson 2

A Circle.

1 book / (pen)

2 computer / notebook

3 book / lesson

4 pen / board

5 lesson / computer

6 board / notebook

B Join the dots and write.

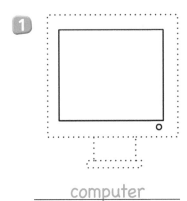

1 computer

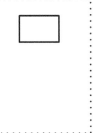

2 _____

3 I am, you are
he is, she is

_____

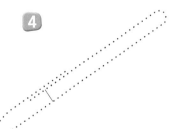

4 _____

5 _____

C **Write There isn't or There aren't.**

1 ___There aren't___ any computers.
2 _____ a drawing in the book.
3 _____ any notebooks for the boys.
4 _____ an animal in the drawing.
5 _____ any pens for the pupils.

D **Write.**

1 ___Is there___ a board in the classroom?   Yes, ___there is___ .
2 _____ pupils in the classroom?   No, _____ .
3 _____ a drawing on the board?   No, _____ .
4 _____ birds in the nest?   Yes, _____ .
5 _____ a tree on the beach?   No, _____ .
6 _____ notebooks on the desks?   Yes, _____ .

E **Write and say.**

| Are there   Is there   There are   ~~There's~~ |

There's a school for you.
___There's___ a school for you.
_____ a school for me?

There are books for you.
_____ books for you.
_____ any books for me?

Hooray! Hooray!
Hooray! Hooray!
Let's go to school today!

Lesson 3

A Circle.

1

(apple) / rubber

2

chair / desk

3

teacher / classroom

4

rubber / ruler

5

classroom / chair

6

teacher / apple

B Tick (✔) or cross (✗).

1 The teacher is in the classroom. ✔

2 There's a chair for the teacher.

3 There are three pupils in the classroom.

4 There are three desks for the pupils.

5 There's a ruler and a rubber on a desk.

6 There's an apple for the teacher.

38

C Circle.

1 There's the / (a) notebook on the chair. The notebook is small.
2 There is an apple in my bag. An / The apple is green!
3 Look! The / A spider! The spider is big and black.
4 I've got a ruler and the / a rubber. The rubber is on my desk.
5 Is there a computer in the classroom? Yes, there is. The / A computer is for the teacher.

D Write a, an or the.

1 There's ____an____ apple on the desk. Is the apple for you?
2 This is a chair. _____ chair is for my friend.
3 There's _____ ruler on the desk. The ruler is blue.
4 Look! _____ helicopter! The helicopter is big!
5 There's a man. Is _____ man a teacher?

E Write, draw and say.

1

look / pencil / green
Look! A pencil.
The pencil is green.

3
look / apple / red
_____
_____

2

look / chair / brown
_____
_____

4
look / rubber / yellow
_____
_____

5 Lesson 1

A **Write.**

1 n <u>o s e</u>

2 e _ r

3 _ y _

4 t _ _ _ _

B **Find, circle and write.**

```
K A N G A R O O
A K O A L A C A
N E S R W P C I
G Y E Y E O A L
A I O A T I O T
X W M E A R S U
R D K T I L E P
O E T E L O N G
```

ear

_____

_____

_____

_____

_____

C Write.

He's got   I̶t̶'̶s̶ ̶g̶o̶t̶   I've got   She's got   You've got

___It's got___ a long tail!

_____ a big robot.

_____ two teddy bears!

_____ three notebooks.

_____ a nice computer!

D Write.

1   I have got green eyes.
   ___I've got___ green eyes.

2   It has got big ears!
   _____ big ears.

3   It has got a long tail!
   _____ a long tail!

4   You have got a big house!
   _____ a big house!

5   She has got one sister.
   _____ one sister.

E Write and say. Then draw.

Thr _e e_ gr _ _ _ n tr _ _ _ s

41

Lesson 2

A Circle.

opo(hair)refdarmooitoemasfingereflegiesadnepwethjk

B Circle.

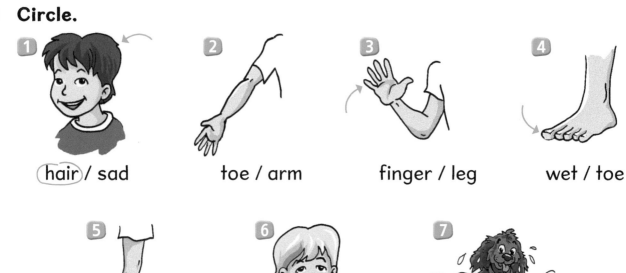

1 (hair)/ sad

2 toe / arm

3 finger / leg

4 wet / toe

5 leg / hair

6 arm / sad

7 wet / finger

C Write.

1 They've got short _____hair_____ .

2 They've got long _____ .

3 They've got eight _____ .

4 They've got ten _____ .

D **Write.**

They've got long tails.   We've got two arms.
You've got brown eyes.   ~~You've got black hair.~~

1

_____You've got black hair._____

3

_____

2

_____

4

_____

E **Write and say.**

eyes   mum   ~~short~~   tall

I'm Sally. I'm short. I've got _____short_____ hair and brown eyes.

This is my _____, Anna. She's _____.
She's got long hair and blue _____.

A **Write.**

B **Match.**

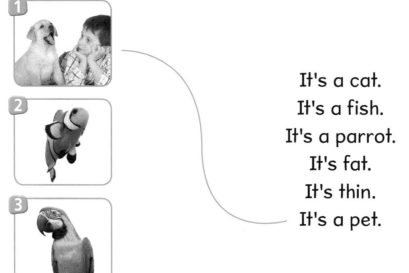

It's a cat.
It's a fish.
It's a parrot.
It's fat.
It's thin.
It's a pet.

C **Write hasn't or haven't.**

1 Snakes _____haven't_____ got one eye.

2 A frog _____ got big ears.

3 A fish _____ got arms and legs.

4 A koala _____ got a long tail.

5 Kangaroos _____ got long hair.

6 Dogs _____ three legs.

D **Write.**

1 I have not got blue eyes.
   I ___haven't got___ blue eyes.

2 We have not got a pet.
   We _____ a pet.

3 My parrot has not got a long tail.
   My parrot _____ a long tail.

4 A fish has not got legs!
   A fish _____ legs!

5 The teachers have not got computers.
   The teachers _____ computers.

6 An octopus has not got toes.
   An octopus _____ toes.

E **Read and draw.**

This is my pet. It's a parrot.
It's red and green. It's got
a long tail!

This is my pet. It's a cat.
It's black and white. It's fat!

This is my pet. It's
a fish. It's orange.
It's small!

Lesson 1

A Write.

m <u>a</u> <u>p</u>

f _ i _ p _ _ s

_ a _ k

m _ _ i _ e p _ o _ e

b _ g

b _ au _ _ f _ l

B Write.

C Circle.

1 Have / (Has) it got beautiful eyes?
2 Have / Has he got a brother or a sister?
3 Have / Has they got a pet?
4 Have / Has Mum got an apple for me?
5 Have / Has Andrew and Tony got a computer?
6 Have / Has the teachers got drawings in the classroom?

D Write.

1 __Have__ you __got__ flippers?   Yes, __I have__ .
2 _____ we _____ bags?   No, _____ .
3 _____ he _____ red hair?   No, _____ .
4 _____ she _____ a map?   Yes, _____ .
5 _____ they _____ a pet?   No, _____ .
6 _____ Jim _____ an apple?   Yes, _____ .

E Write and say.

Has he got a bike?
Yes, he has.

Has she got a map?
_____

Have they got bags?
_____

Has she got flippers?
_____

Have they got a pet?
_____

Have we got a mask?
_____

Lesson 2

A **Circle.**

1

dancer / (skirt)

2

shoes / jacket

3

shirt / clothes

4

socks / dancer

5

socks / shoes

6

clothes / jacket

7

shirt / skirt

B **Write.**

1 _s_ h i _r_ t

2 j _ _ k _ t

3 s _ i _ t

4 b _ _ _

5 _ o c _ s

6 s _ _ _ e s

48

C Write.

The ___boy's shirt___ is blue.

The _____ is pink.

_____ is red.

The _____ is yellow.

D Write.

1 skirt / Jane's / is / beautiful

Jane's skirt is beautiful. _____

2 small / the / shoes / are / dancer's

_____

3 fantastic / the / birthday cake / girl's / is

_____

4 white / boy's / is / shirt / the

_____

5 shoes / blue / John's / are

_____

E Read, draw and say.

a crazy hat

funny socks

cool shoes

Lesson 3

A **Find, circle and write.**

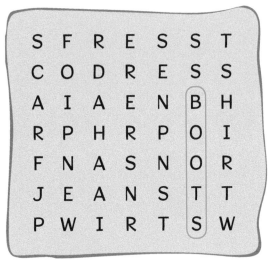

S	F	R	E	S	S	T
C	O	D	R	E	S	S
A	I	A	E	N	B	H
R	P	H	R	P	O	I
F	N	A	S	N	O	R
J	E	A	N	S	T	T
P	W	I	R	T	S	W

 1

boots

 4

_____

 2

_____

 5

_____

 3

_____

 6

_____

B **Read and draw.**

1

a pink and blue T-shirt

2

blue jeans

3

brown boots

4

a green and yellow scarf

5

a purple and orange dress

50

C Circle.

1 They've got a new house. (Their) / Our house is fantastic!
2 I've got a pet. This is her / my dog Bobby.
3 We're boys. We love our / your skateboards!
4 I'm John. What's their / your name?
5 Peter has got a book in her / his bag.
6 Anna's skirt is blue and its / her jacket is too.

D Write.

We're sisters. This is ___our___ pet cat.

I'm Sam. This is _____ new scarf.

They're brothers. _____ names are Ben and Rick.

My name's Emma. What's _____ name?

E Read and draw. Then say.

My name's Jane. My jeans are blue. My t-shirt is pink. My scarf is yellow and my boots are black. I'm cool!

Review 2

A Write.

apple bag book board chair computer desk
mobile phone notebook pen pupil rubber ruler ~~teacher~~

1	teacher	8	
2		9	
3		10	
4		11	
5		12	
6		13	
7		14	

B Circle.

My name's Trek and these are my reporters! I have got brown (1) legs / hair. I am (2) thin / fat. I have got a blue (3) skirt / shirt, blue (4) jeans / boots and green (5) socks / shoes. Ty is a panda! He is (6) fat / thin and he has got a short (7) ear / tail. Leo is a leopard! He has got four (8) legs / eyes and a Mia is a meerkat! She has got two (9) fingers / ears and she is (10) sad / beautiful.

C Write.

Are there Is there There are There aren't ~~There's~~ There isn't

1 Look! ___There's___ a kangaroo!

2 _____ any apples.

3 _____ any books? No, there aren't.

4 _____ eleven boys in the classroom.

5 _____ a monkey in the tree? Yes, there is.

6 _____ a dress. There's a skirt.

D Write.

1 __Have__ you __got__ a pet? Yes, I __have__ .

2 Ben _____ (✗) a cat. He's got a parrot.

3 I _____ (✔) a jacket. It is blue.

4 Lucy and John _____ (✗) flippers. They have got a mask.

5 _____ he _____ a lesson? No, he _____ .

6 You _____ (✔) two eyes. Your eyes are blue.

E Circle.

1 We've got fish. Their /(Our) fish are orange.

2 I've got a parrot. My / Her parrot is red and green.

3 He's got a T-shirt. Her / His T-shirt is blue.

4 They've got a new teacher. Their / My teacher is Mrs Black.

5 Penny's got a new dress. Its / Her dress is nice.

6 The dog's got a ball. Our / Its ball is yellow.

F Write and match.

1 blue / is / mask / Pete's
   __Pete's mask is blue.__

2 parrot / red / is / Mum's
   _____

3 long / the / tail / cat's / is
   _____

4 Sarah's / beautiful / is / dress
   _____

53

Lesson 1

A Circle.

1
jump / swim

2
run / look at

3
play volleyball / sea

4
play volleyball / swim

5
look at / run

6
sea / jump

B Write.

jump ~~look at~~ play volleyball run swim sea

1
_____Look at_____
Jane's cat.

2
The dolphins are in
the _____ .

3
She can
_____ .

4
Kangaroos can
_____ .

5
The children can
_____ .

6
A ball! Let's
_____!

C **Circle.**

1 He's a baby. He can / (can't) read.
2 Bill can / can't play volleyball. He hasn't got a ball.
3 Tigers can / can't run.
4 Oh no! Tina can / can't dance!
5 Dolphins can / can't swim.
6 My brother's cool. He can / can't swim.

D **Write.**

Jane	✗	✗	✗	✔
Rick	✗	✔	✔	✔

1 Rick _____can_____ jump.
2 Jane _____ swim.
3 Jane and Rick _____ run.
4 Rick _____ swim.
5 Jane _____ jump.
6 Jane and Rick _____ dance.

E **Write and say.**

Dance everybody! We can dance.
Dance everybody! We can d <u>a</u> n <u>c e</u>.

Sit down, stand up.
We can clap our hands!
Sit down, s _ _ n _ up.
We can clap our _ a _ d _ !

Jump left, jump r _ _ _ ht.
You _ a _ clap your hands!
Jump left, j _ _ _ p right.
You can clap your hands!

Lesson 2

A **Join the dots and write.**

1

2

3

recorder _____ _____

4

5

_____ _____

B **Write.**

C Match.

1 Can Phil dance?

2 Can Natalie sing?

3 Can birds swim?

4 Can John play the drums?

5 Can Alice swim?

6 Can Mike and Joe play volleyball?

a No, they can't.

b Yes, he can.

c No, she can't.

d Yes, she can.

e Yes, they can.

f Yes, he can.

D Write about you.

1 Can you swim?   _____

2 Can you play the drums?   _____

3 Can you play volleyball?   _____

4 Can you sing?   _____

5 Can you play the recorder?   _____

6 Can you play the piano?   _____

E Write and draw.

This is my best friend.

_____ name is _____ .

_____ can _____ .

_____ can't _____ .

Lesson 3

A Match.

1 play   music

2 ride   TV

3 listen to   a book

4 watch   the guitar

5 read   a bike

a

b

c

d

e

B Write.

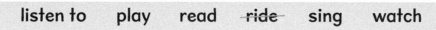

listen to   play   read   ~~ride~~   sing   watch

I can _____ride_____ a bike.

He can _____ music.

I can _____ books.

She can _____ songs.

He can _____ TV.

They can _____ the recorder.

C **Write.**

1   I am reading a book
    _____I'm reading_____ a book.

2   Look! She is dancing.
    Look! _____ .

3   You are listening to music.
    _____ to music.

4   Look at the cat! It is running.
    Loot at the cat! _____ .

5   He is riding a bike.
    _____ a bike.

6   Wow! They are singing a song.
    Wow! _____ a song.

D **Write.**

1   Grandpa _____is watching_____ (watch) TV.
2   I _____ (play) the drums.
3   You _____ (sing) a song.
4   Spot the dog _____ (look at) a cat.
5   Pat _____ (read) a book.
6   I _____ (ride) my bike.

E **Write and say.**

1   _____He is playing the drums._____
2   _____
3   _____
4   _____
5   _____
6   _____

59

Lesson 1

A Match.

tennis
baseball
win
think
football
basketball

B Find, circle and write.

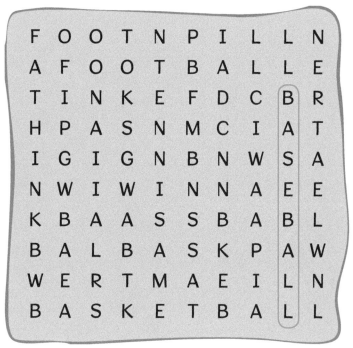

baseball _____

_____

_____

_____

_____

_____

C **Write.**

> They're playing basketball. ~~They're playing football.~~
> We're riding our bikes. We're watching TV.
> You're playing the piano. You're singing a song.

1. They're playing football.

2. _____

3. _____

4. _____

5. _____

6. _____

D **Write.**

1 They are jumping.
   They're jumping .

2 We are playing football.
   _____ football.

3 You are swimming in the sea.
   _____ in the sea.

4 We are singing a song.
   _____ a song.

5 They are listening to music.
   _____ to music.

6 You are playing the drums.
   _____ the drums.

E **Join the dots. Then write and say.**

Th _ y a _ e p _ a _ ing
bas _ et _ _ ll.

Lesson 2

A Circle.

sittagrollercoastermponstanddewoldvpeopleertownfyh

B Write.

old   people   rollercoaster   sit   stand   town

1
_____ stand _____

2
_____

3
_____

4
_____

5
_____

6
_____

C Circle.

1   I **'m** / aren't listening to music.

2   My friends isn't / **aren't** playing computer games.

3   He **isn't** / aren't standing. He's sitting!

4   They isn't / **aren't** riding the rollercoaster.

5   You **aren't** / isn't looking at me!

6   She aren't / **isn't** watching the basketball.

62

D Match.

1   Maria isn't eating a birthday cake.   [d]
2   Barry isn't playing football.   ☐
3   They aren't drawing a flower.   ☐
4   The dogs aren't playing with a red ball.   ☐
5   The girls aren't walking.   ☐
6   The monkey isn't swimming.   ☐

E Write and say.

R o l l e r c o a s t e r s are great!
_ o _ l _ r _ o _ s _ e _ s are cool!
Come on, everybody.
Let's have some fun.

Up, up, _ p we go.
_ o _ k _ t us.
Down, down, _ o _ n we go.
L _ o _ a _ us.

We are riding the rollercoaster.
We are having _ u _ .
Come on, everybody.
Put your h _ n _ s up.

Rollercoasters are fun!

Lesson 3

A Circle.

1

(climb) / dance

2

cook / kick

3

dance / rock

4

kick / cook

5

rock / climb

B Match.

1

2

3

Jane's riding her bike.

Helen's making a cake.

Mario's climbing a rock.

Paul's kicking a ball

Steve's dancing.

Anne's climbing a tree.

4

5

6

C Circle.

1 Are the birds flying?
(Yes, they are.) / No, they aren't.

2 Is the cat climbing the tree?
Yes, it is. / No, it isn't.

3 Are Mum and Dad sitting?
Yes, they are. / No, they aren't.

4 Is Dad cooking?
Yes, he is. / No, he isn't.

5 Is the dog looking at the cat?
Yes, it is. / No, it isn't.

6 Is Simon reading a book?
Yes, he is. / No, he isn't.

D Match.

1 Are you playing the drums?   a Yes, we are.
2 Is Timothy climbing the rock?   b No, I'm not.
3 Is the kangaroo jumping?   c No, it isn't.
4 Are we playing basketball?   d Yes, he is.
5 Are the boys having fun?   e No, they aren't

E Write and say.

Lisa

Tom

Penny

Anna

Paula

Harry

1 He isn't sitting. He's running.   It's Tom.
2 She isn't cooking. She's playing the guitar.   _____
3 She isn't playing tennis. She's reading a book.   _____
4 He isn't playing the guitar. He's swimming.   _____
5 She isn't running. She's cooking.   _____
6 She isn't swimming. She's playing tennis.   _____

A Write.

1 <u>t h e a t r e</u>
2 c _ _ _ _ a
3 _ _ r k _ _
4 _ _ _ t

B Write.

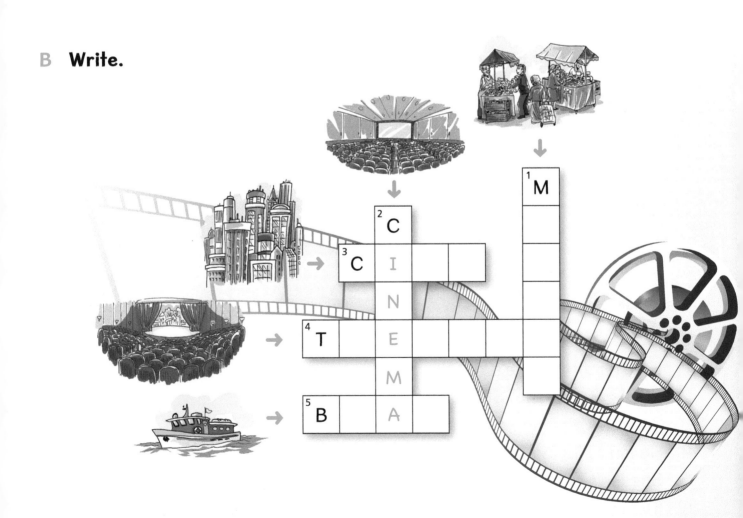

C Match.

1 What is Mary doing?
2 What is John doing?
3 What are the boys doing?
4 What am I doing?
5 What are you doing?

a They're playing volleyball.
b He's riding his bike.
c I'm reading my book.
d She's playing the piano.
e You're swimming in the sea.

D Write.

What are they doing?   What are you doing?   ~~What are you doing?~~
What's it doing?   What's she doing?   What's he doing?

What are you doing?
I'm climbing a tree!

_____
She's reading a book.

_____
They are cooking!

_____
It's eating its food.

_____
He's thinking.

_____
We're swimming.

E Write and say.

T h is is my brother.
He's ___ ___ in.

Lesson 2

A   Match.

1

dragon
colours
fireworks
sky

3

4

B   Write.

Dance!   Don't look!   ~~Jump!~~   Kick!   Look!   Run!

1   Jump!

2

3

4

5

6

C Write.

colours   dragon   fireworks   ~~New Year~~   sky

1   _____New Year_____ in China is great!
2   What is the _____ doing? It's dancing.
3   The _____ in the sky are beautiful!
4   Blue, red and green are _____ .
5   Look! Birds are flying in the _____!

D Match and write.

1   Don't play the guitar!   a   _____ basketball!
2   Cook a birthday cake!   b   _____ a tree.
3   Don't sit on the bed!   c   _____ on the chair!
4   Don't climb a mountain!   d   _____Play_____ the piano!
5   Swim in the sea.   e   _____ in a river.
6   Play volleyball!   f   _____ eggs.

E Write and say.

F <u>i</u> r e w <u>o</u> r <u>k</u> s in the s __ y!
Whizz! Pop! Whoosh!
Red and blue, yellow and green.
Whizz! Pop! Whoosh!

It's N __ w __ e __ r today.
Hooray! Hooray! Hooray!
It's __ e __ Y __ a __ today.
Hooray! Hooray! Hooray

69

A Circle.

barivertparknbgnbuylomcshopdepicnicksIridehocthingyws

B Write.

buy   ~~park~~   picnic   river   shop

1

Hooray! Let's go to the _____park_____ .

2

They are having a _____ .

3

Let's go on a boat ride on the _____ .

4

Mum can _____ food.

5

There is a _____ in the city.

C Match.

1 Let's play
2 Let's buy
3 Let's have
4 Let's go
5 Let's swim
6 Let's watch

a a party.
b presents.
c in the river.
d on a bus ride.
e the fireworks.
f football.

D Write.

| Let's buy | Let's go | Let's have | Let's look | Let's ride | Let's sit |

__Let's go__
to the theatre.

_____
a picnic.

_____
Grandma a present.

_____
at the toys.

_____
the rollercoaster.

_____
on the chairs.

E Join the dots. Then write and say.

L e t'_ d _ _ _ _ e!

Review 3

A Find, circle and write.

```
T E N N I S Y Q B M Y
H J B A S E B A L L Y
E T A D R C L F O M A
A G S Y E O I O H F L
T U K T C Z Y O C W I
R I E M O F D T I P R
E T T A R I R B N A P
U A B R D K U A E R I
G R A K E W M L M K A
X L L E R U S L A M N
A Z L T Y P M G L T O
```

City

cinema
_____
_____
_____

Music

_____
_____
_____
_____

Sport

_____
_____
_____
_____
_____

B Write.

1 ____Let's read!____
2 _____
3 _____
4 _____
5 _____
6 _____
7 _____
8 _____

C Write.

1 ____Are they running____ (they / run)? Yes, they are.

2 I _____ (play) volleyball.

3 She _____ (not read) a book.

4 _____ (he / swim) in the sea? No, he isn't.

5 We _____ (listen) to music.

72

D Write.

1 _____Can_____ the shark swim? __Yes__, it _____can_____ . (✔)
   _____Can_____ it read? No, __it can't__ . (✗)

2 The old people _____ ride a bike. (✗) They _____ watch TV. (✔)

3 The kangaroo _____ jump. (✔) It _____ cook. (✗)

4 _____ the boy play volleyball? _____, he _____ . (✔)
   _____ the boy play the piano? _____, he _____. (✗)

5 The teacher _____ sing. (✗) She _____ listen to music. (✔)

6 I _____ run. (✔) I _____ dance. (✗)

E Match.

1 What are you doing?
2 What's it doing?
3 What are they doing?
4 What are you doing?
5 What's he doing?
6 What's she doing?

a It's jumping.
b I'm thinking.
c They're cooking.
d We're watching TV.
e She's playing the guitar.
f He's playing volleyball.

F Write about you.

My name is _____ .
I can _____ .
I can't _____ .

Lesson 1

A Circle.

1. (living room) / kitchen

2. reporter / glass

3. man / glass

4. bedroom / living room

5. glass / reporter

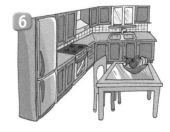
6. kitchen / bedroom

B Write.

bedroom   glass   ~~kitchen~~   living room   man   reporter

1. Dad is cooking in the ____kitchen____ .

2. Mum's watching TV in the _____ .

3. The _____ has got a baby.

4. Bill's mum is a _____ .

5. The girls are playing in their _____ .

6. Penny is drinking a _____ of milk.

74

C **Write.**

baby	babies
	beaches
bus	
	children
foot	
	foxes
glass	
	men
tomato	
	women

D **Count and write.**

1

two men

2

_____

3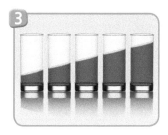

_____

4

_____

5

_____

6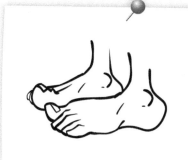

_____

E **Read and draw.**

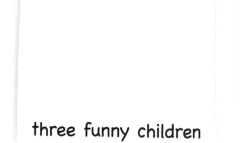

two big feet

three funny children

four red tomatoes

Lesson 2

A **Join the dots and write.**

1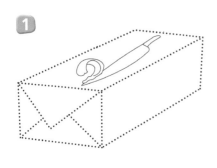

2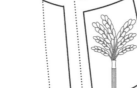

3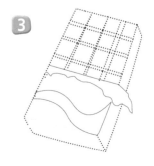

____butter____

_____

_____

4

5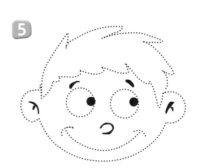

_____

_____

B **Write.**

1 f l o u r

2 m _ l _

3 _ u _ t _ r

4 e _ g _

5 _ h _ c _ l _ t _

C   Circle.

1   Have you got (any)/ some chocolate?
2   We've got any / some cake.
3   I have got any / some milk.
4   Have you got any / some eggs?
5   I haven't got any / some apples.
6   Dad has got any / some books.

D   Write some or any.

1   Have we got _____any_____ chocolate?
2   There are _____ cakes in the kitchen.
3   I've got _____ sugar.
4   Mark hasn't got _____ friends.
5   Jane's got _____ flour on her nose!
6   Are there _____ trees in the park?

E   Write and say.

Rub your tummy.
Rub your tummy.
m i l k and _ h _ c _ l _ t _ today!

Rub your tummy.
Rub your tummy.
M _ l _ and c _ k _ s today!

Yummy, yummy, yummy!
Come on rub your tummy!
Yummy, yummy, yummy!

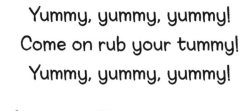

77

Lesson 3

A Find, circle and write.

B	S	C	H	E	E	S	E
A	D	G	C	H	N	W	U
S	O	R	A	N	G	E	W
K	R	F	R	O	Q	E	T
E	C	B	R	J	V	T	K
T	D	E	O	I	P	S	M
A	P	O	T	A	T	O	L

1 _____   4 _____
   basket

2 _____   5 _____

3 _____   6 _____

B Write.

1 I've got some  _____sweets_____ .

2 Mum has got the _____ .

3 I've got a  _____ .

4 We haven't got any _____ .

5 Don't eat sweets! Eat an _____ .

6 There is a _____ in Mum's basket.

C Circle.

1   Sally is (behind) / next to John.

2   The apple is in / on the table.

3   The red car is in front of / in the yellow car.

4   The girl is next to / under the table.

5   The family are on / in their car.

6   The rabbit is behind / next to the tree.

D Write.

behind	in	in front of	~~next to~~	on	under

1   Where's the cinema?
    It's _____next to_____ the theatre.

2   Where are the children?
    They're _____ the car.

3   Where's the bike?
    It's _____ the tree.

4   Where's the mouse?
    It's _____ the cat.

5   Where's the guitar?
    It's _____ the chair.

6   Where's the bag?
    It's _____ the desk.

E Read and draw.

There is a big tree in front of my house. There are red flowers on the tree. There's a big basket under the tree. There are some apples in the basket. My bike is behind the tree. I'm standing next to my bike.

Lesson 1

A Write.

Friday ~~Monday~~ Saturday Sunday Thursday Tuesday Wednesday

S u n d a y
M _ _ _ _ _ _
T _ _ _ _ _ _ _
W _ _ _ _ _ _ _ _ _
T _ _ _ _ _ _ _
F _ _ _ _ _ _
S _ _ _ _ _ _ _ _

B Write.

SUNDAY	MONDAY	TUESDAY	WEDNESDAY	THURSDAY	FRIDAY	SATURDAY

1 Sarah has a picnic on _____Saturday_____!

2 Sarah plays computer games on _____ .

3 Sarah has drawing lessons on _____ .

4 Sarah has piano lessons on _____ .

5 Sarah plays volleyball on _____ .

6 Sarah swims on _____ .

7 Sarah has dance lessons on _____ .

C Circle.

1 Billy ride / (rides) his bike to school.
2 She watch / watches football on TV.
3 I love / loves guitar lessons!
4 Tom work / works in a toy shop.
5 Anita go / goes to English lessons on Wednesday.
6 He play / plays football in the park.

D Write.

1 Helen _____loves_____ (love) basketball!
2 I _____ (go) to the shops on Saturday.
3 Pat _____ (play) football on Friday!
4 She _____ (swim) in the river!
5 I _____ (buy) my clothes in town.
6 He _____ (sing) great songs!

E Write and say.

S _u_ n _d_ a _y_ is OK.
_ o _ d _ y is OK.
_ u _ s _ a _ is good,
    I say!

But Friday is great,
And Saturday is fantastic.
They're the best days,
    I say!

W _ d _ e _ d _ y is OK.
_ h _ r _ d _ y is OK.
All the days are good,
    I say.

F _ i _ a _ and Saturday.
Friday and _ a _ u _ d _ y.
I love Friday and Saturday!

A Write.

w _e_ _a_ r

2

_ _ e _ _ f _ _ t

3

_ _ t

4

_ a _ t _ e

5

g _ _ _ _ p

6

s _ _ w

B Find, circle and write.

A	Q	I	C	R	L	E	E	F
B	R	E	A	K	F	A	S	T
W	J	O	S	F	M	T	N	Y
N	G	E	T	U	P	X	O	B
S	K	P	L	T	A	U	W	V
B	C	W	E	A	R	Z	D	G

1

_____wear_____

4

_____

2

_____

5

_____

3

_____

6

_____

C **Match.**

1 We play
2 You eat
3 They read
4 We watch
5 They swim
6 You ride

a in the park.
b TV in the living room.
c eggs for breakfast.
d in the sea
e books.
f a bicycle.

D **Write.**

They play   We love   We read   ~~You climb~~

1 _____You climb_____ trees!

3 _____ cakes.

2 _____ the guitar.

4 _____ books.

E **Write and say.**

lessons   ~~love~~   picnic   Sunday

I _____love_____ Wednesday
and Saturday.
On Wednesday I have dance
_____ .
On _____ we have
a _____ !

Lesson 3

A Circle.

1

(crisps) / popcorn

2

scooter / maths

3

maths / popcorn

4

crisps / scooter

B Write.

crisps   English   live   ~~maths~~   popcorn   scooter

1 I love ___maths___ .

4 There is a _____ behind that tree!

2 We watch TV and eat _____ .

5 We _____ in Africa.

3 I like _____ .

6 _____ is my favourite lesson.

C **Write.**

1 My sister likes crisps. She _____doesn't like_____ popcorn.
2 John rides a scooter. He _____ a bicycle.
3 I like English. I _____ maths.
4 Jane watches TV. She _____ DVDs.
5 My dad plays the guitar. He _____ the drums.
6 I drink orange juice. I _____ milk.

D **Match.**

Jim doesn't play the drums.
My brother doesn't eat crisps.
Dad doesn't ride a bicycle.
Mum doesn't drink milk.
They don't swim in the sea.
Mark doesn't play basketball.

E **Write.**

carrots   ~~popcorn~~   school   swimming

He likes _____popcorn_____ .
He doesn't like _____ .

She likes _____ .
She doesn't like _____ .

A Match.

1

2

3

4

5

6

cave
goat
island
moon
panda
sun

B Write.

C Circle.

1 Does the cat eat carrots?
   No, it doesn't / No, they don't.

2 Do the children have lessons on Sunday?
   No, you don't. / No, they don't.

3 Do goats eat flowers?
   Yes, they do. / Yes, it does.

4 Do you love carrots?
   No, it doesn't. / No, we don't.

5 Does George work on Saturday?
   Yes, he does. / Yes, she does.

6 Does Emma like sweets?
   Yes, she does. / Yes, I do.

D Write about you.

1 Do you like sweets? _____

2 Does your mum like dogs? _____

3 Do your friends go to school? _____

4 Do you read books? _____

5 Does your dad work on Saturday? _____

6 Do you like carrots? _____

E Write and say.

Helen

George

Billy

Susie

Joe and Katie

1 Does George like climbing? ___Yes, he does.___

2 Does Billy like goats? _____

3 Does Helen like cakes? _____

4 Does Susie like reading? _____

5 Do Joe and Katie like school? _____

Lesson 2

A Circle.

1 **afternoon** / night

2 study / go to bed

3 laugh / go to bed

4 night / afternoon

5 night / morning

6 study / laugh

B Write.

1 Do you have breakfast in the  _____morning_____?

2 Does your mum work in the  _____?

3 Do you  _____ on Fridays?

4 Does your brother  _____ at 8 o'clock?

5 Do you sleep at  _____?

6 Do you _____ a lot?

88

C Match.

1 What does your mum do in the morning?

2 What do your friends do every day?

3 What do you do in the evening?

4 What do you and your sister do at the weekend?

5 What does your dad do in the afternoon?

a I play basketball.

b He listens to music.

c We play tennis.

d They go to school.

e She cooks breakfast.

D Write do or does.

1 What _____do_____ they do at night?

2 What _____ Carol do in the morning?

3 What _____ you do in the park?

4 What _____ Michael do every afternoon?

5 What _____ they do at 4 o'clock?

6 What _____ Helen do every day?

E Write and say.

bed   eat   ~~get up~~   go   run

Get up! Get up!
Sleepy head!
____Get up____! Get up!
Jump out of bed!

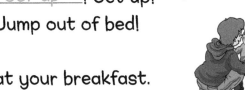

Eat your breakfast.
_____ it all!
Eat your breakfast.
Go to school!

Run home! Run home!
Let's play a game.
Run home! _____ home!
Let's climb a tree.

Go to bed.
Go to _____ .
Sleepy head.
_____ to bed.

A Circle.

It's spring / (autumn)!

It's hot / cold.

It's winter / summer!

It's cold / hot!

It's autumn / winter!

It's summer / spring!

B Find, circle and write.

S	P	R	I	N	G	A	S	Q
U	H	E	G	F	E	U	G	M
M	I	B	W	I	N	T	E	R
M	J	H	C	D	P	U	A	T
E	C	O	L	D	D	M	S	V
R	K	T	L	M	O	N	X	C

1

spring

4

_____

2

_____

5

_____

3

_____

6

_____

C Write.

What   When   Where   Who

1 ____What____ is your favourite season?
Summer.
2 _____ do you play with your friends?
In the afternoon.
3 _____ are those people in the bus?
My friends!
4 _____ does Phillip's dad work?
In a computer shop.

D Circle and match.

1 (Who)/ What is that girl?   a Chocolate!
2 When / What is your favourite food?   b Basketball.
3 Where / Who is your school?   c My sister.
4 What / When is your birthday?   d At work.
5 What / Where is you mum?   e In Cairo.
6 When / What is your favourite sport? f 21st May.

E Match and say.

Where do you live?

6 o'clock.

Who is that man?

In Egypt.

When do you get up for school?

Saturday.

What is your favourite day?

My dad.

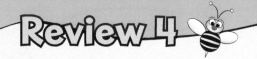
Units 10-12

A **Write.**

autumn   bedroom   butter   castle   chocolate   kitchen
living room   ~~Monday~~   orange   potato   spring   summer
Sunday   Thursday   Wednesday   winter

Days	Food	House	Seasons
Monday			

B **Write.**

C **Circle.**

1   On Monday Mum go / (goes) to work.

2   They watch / watches TV in the bedroom.

3   Penny don't swim / doesn't swim on Fridays.

4   Do they live / Does they live in a castle?

5   John don't like / doesn't like carrots.

6   Do we play / Does we play tennis on Friday?

D **Write.**

behind   in   in front of   next to   ~~on~~   under

1 The flowers are _____on_____ the table.
2 The boy is _____ the girls.
3 The dog is _____ the cat.
4 The presents are _____ the tree.
5 The brown goat is _____ the white goat.
6 The oranges are _____ the basket.

E **Write.**

1 ? / is / your / what / day / favourite   _What day is your favourite?_
2 any / I / popcorn / got / haven't   _____
3 ? / that / is / girl / who   _____
4 ? / school / where / their / is   _____
5 ? / got / any / carrots / have / we   _____
6 some / chocolate / got / I've   _____

F **Write about you.**

On Sundays, I _____ .
On Mondays, I _____ .
On Tuesdays, I _____ .
On Wednesdays, I _____ .
On Thursdays, I _____ .
On Fridays, I _____ .
On Saturdays, I _____ .

Wordsearches

Unit 1

Find, circle and write 12 words from Unit 1.

```
T  B  R  O  T  H  E  R  B  B
O  K  F  A  M  I  L  Y  E  A
X  G  R  A  N  D  P  A  S  B
G  E  O  E  R  H  C  N  T  Y
R  C  S  I  S  T  E  R  F  U
A  W  I  G  L  O  O  D  R  A
N  F  E  N  R  A  W  T  I  C
D  V  P  H  O  T  O  A  E  M
M  D  A  D  F  A  Y  B  N  U
A  Z  H  O  U  S  E  R  D  M
```

1 _____ baby
2 _____
3 _____
4 _____
5 _____
6 _____
7 _____
8 _____
9 _____
10 _____
11 _____
12 _____

Unit 2

Find, circle and write 12 words from Unit 2.

```
D  T  D  S  S  H  O  R  T  T
S  T  X  K  L  I  O  N  N  T
M  K  S  A  B  A  L  L  E  E
A  R  O  T  T  O  Y  A  E  D
L  P  R  E  S  E  N  T  C  D
L  H  G  B  M  R  F  A  A  Y
S  R  S  O  V  T  E  L  M  B
G  I  R  A  F  F  E  L  E  E
A  P  A  R  T  Y  W  W  R  A
B  I  F  D  H  A  P  T  A  R
```

1 _____ ball
2 _____
3 _____
4 _____
5 _____
6 _____
7 _____
8 _____
9 _____
10 _____
11 _____
12 _____

94

Unit 3

Find, circle and write 12 words from Unit 3.

```
D B I R D S H A R K
O N P E N G U I N B
L M I Q R A B B I T
P M E E R K A T Y I
H S L O L I P K R O
I N (A N I M A L S) T
N A Y F L O W E R X
W K M O U N T A I N
N E O S T R I C H V
T W H A L E Y D G M
```

1 _____ animals _____
2 _____
3 _____
4 _____
5 _____
6 _____
7 _____
8 _____
9 _____
10 _____
11 _____
12 _____

Unit 4

Find, circle and write 12 words from Unit 4.

```
L N O T E B O O K T
H E L I C O V T E R
O B C X L Y X E W S
W O O C A L R A S P
R A M H S E U C C E
U R P A S S B H H N
L D U I R S B E O C
E N T R O O E R O I
R G E A O N R Q L L
S S R E M B D E S K
```

1 _____ board _____
2 _____
3 _____
4 _____
5 _____
6 _____
7 _____
8 _____
9 _____
10 _____
11 _____
12 _____

Wordsearches

Find, circle and write 12 words from Unit 5.

S	A	D	T	D	P	H	A	I	R
V	L	E	G	E	A	I	P	B	M
M	F	W	E	T	R	F	A	T	W
E	O	R	A	G	R	I	B	O	J
T	S	L	S	L	O	N	G	E	H
H	H	M	J	F	T	G	N	Y	C
I	V	T	A	I	L	E	R	E	A
N	E	A	R	M	A	R	M	C	T
C	X	N	O	S	E	W	X	V	R
D	Q	K	E	N	L	A	B	G	E

1 _____ arm _____
2 _____
3 _____
4 _____
5 _____
6 _____
7 _____
8 _____
9 _____
10 _____
11 _____
12 _____

Unit 6

Find, circle and write 12 words from Unit 6.

M	G	K	C	L	O	T	H	E	S
I	A	S	H	I	R	T	B	A	G
S	J	S	B	O	O	T	S	P	U
K	F	U	T	P	P	E	R	S	T
S	O	C	K	S	C	A	R	F	S
S	J	A	C	K	E	T	F	Q	H
K	M	A	P	J	E	A	N	S	I
I	L	V	D	A	K	C	T	R	R
R	D	R	E	S	S	Y	E	B	T
T	N	E	X	S	H	O	E	S	O

1 _____ bag _____
2 _____
3 _____
4 _____
5 _____
6 _____
7 _____
8 _____
9 _____
10 _____
11 _____
12 _____

Unit 7

Find, circle and write 12 words from Unit 7.

```
X G U Y H M V O O W
N U F Y S E S G X J
R I M D O W W X V E
E T I R N S I N G U
A A I U G T M J Q W
D R I M O A R J U A
D M U S I C N C F T
R E C O R D E R K C
J L R U N J U M P H
C S P I A N O H K G
```

1 _____ drums _____
2 _____
3 _____
4 _____
5 _____
6 _____
7 _____
8 _____
9 _____
10 _____
11 _____
12 _____

Unit 8

Find, circle and write 12 words from Unit 8.

```
E L I R T B S D V C
M S T P H R I A X L
Q E O E U O T N B I
M L W O N C E C A M
C N N P K K N E S B
O D K L O W N C E S
O G F E L I I V B E
K I C K D N S D A B
B A S K E T B A L L
F O O T B A L L L E
```

1 _____ baseball _____
2 _____
3 _____
4 _____
5 _____
6 _____
7 _____
8 _____
9 _____
10 _____
11 _____
12 _____

Wordsearches

Unit 9

Find, circle and write 12 words from Unit 9.

H	H	D	R	A	G	O	N	X	T
S	H	O	P	I	C	N	I	C	M
C	C	O	L	O	U	R	S	C	A
T	U	S	P	A	R	K	E	I	R
M	R	A	K	U	L	H	Y	T	K
C	L	R	I	V	E	R	H	Y	E
F	I	R	E	W	O	R	K	S	T
F	T	C	I	N	E	M	A	S	O
M	T	H	E	A	T	R	E	K	D
G	B	O	A	T	B	J	L	Y	M

1 _boat_
2 _____
3 _____
4 _____
5 _____
6 _____
7 _____
8 _____
9 _____
10 _____
11 _____
12 _____

Unit 10

Find, circle and write 12 words from Unit 10.

Y	O	C	H	E	E	S	E	G	B
K	I	T	C	H	E	N	R	W	A
R	G	L	A	S	S	E	R	Q	S
G	V	G	C	A	R	R	O	T	K
C	H	O	C	O	L	A	T	E	E
F	B	U	T	T	E	R	N	H	T
L	J	T	Q	P	O	T	A	T	O
O	V	Q	R	O	R	A	N	G	E
U	Z	F	S	W	E	E	T	S	O
R	I	V	I	N	G	M	I	L	K

1 _basket_
2 _____
3 _____
4 _____
5 _____
6 _____
7 _____
8 _____
9 _____
10 _____
11 _____
12 _____

Unit 11

Find, circle and write 12 words from Unit 11.

```
M D U P O P C O R N
O W E D N E S D A Y
N T S A T U R D A Y
D Q C A S T L E A T
A S N O W U I X M C
Y A V S X E V X O R
W T H U R S D A Y I
M A T H S D M P U S
V S U N D A Y J F P
F R I D A Y G I M S
```

1 castle
2 _____
3 _____
4 _____
5 _____
6 _____
7 _____
8 _____
9 _____
10 _____
11 _____
12 _____

Unit 12

Find, circle and write 12 words from Unit 12.

```
H O T P S P R I N G
D J A C N I G H T A
R S U M M E R B V F
I B T O S T U D P T
T W U R M L C M Z E
O I M N O S O A P R
N N N I O U L V T N
R T N N N D E N O O
L E N G O A T N T O
Y R L O C S Y D A N
```

1 afternoon
2 _____
3 _____
4 _____
5 _____
6 _____
7 _____
8 _____
9 _____
10 _____
11 _____
12 _____